budabebe®

jacquie o'neill

JACQUIE O'NEILL
ILLUSTRATION ltd

budabebe®

www.budabebe.com

**With all my deepest love and affection
I dedicate Budabebe to my four daughters,
Rowan, Abigail, Liberty and Raphaella.
Namaste.**

THIS IS A GREAT BRITISH PRODUCT

Published by Jacquie O'Neill Illustration Ltd
The Old Manse, Camelford, Cornwall, PL32 9XA, England.
ISBN: 978-0-9568233-0-4

Printed in Suffolk, England.

budabebe®

Yoga is excellent for young children,
helping them develop supple healthy
bodies and at the same time nurturing
strong and emotionally sound minds,
resulting in a happy and balanced child.

Yoga poses strengthen and nurture
young muscles and enable your child to
become aware of the self.

Yoga breathing can help your child
control their anger and if you have a shy
child, can provide a confidence boost.

Yoga relaxation can help your child with
rest and sleep which is an essential
building block to a healthy body.

This Budabebe Book belongs to:

Budabebe like a mountain,
stretch up really tall,

Budabebe spread out your arms and legs,
the brightest star of all.

Budabebe balance on one leg,
a green and leafy tree,

Budabebe be a puppet,
bend your head down to your knee.

Budabebe hands down to the floor
and do a bunny hop,

Budabebe straighten out your legs,
you are a downward dog.

Budabebe be a Snow Cat,
arch your back up off the floor.

Budabebe be a lion,
with a loud and fierce roar,

Budabebe be a butterfly,
floating up and down

Budabebe be an owl at night,
and slowly look around

Budabebe curl into a ball,
like little harvest mice

Budabebe think a happy thought, something really nice

Put your happy thoughts here...

and here too.

and here...

Budabebe roll flat on to your back,
in a peaceful silent pose,

Breath in rainbows Budabebe,
see how the colour flows.

Mountain

Stand tall with your feet close together. Inhale as you lift your arms overhead reaching high. Breathe evenly.

Sanskrit Yoga Name:
TADASANA

Star

Stand with your feet together. Inhale and step your legs out to the side as you lift your arms and stretch them out.

Sanskrit Yoga Name:
TRIKONASANA

Tree

Stand tall with feet hip width apart. Lift your right leg and place it on the inside of the left leg (or just lift it into the air) Lift your arms above your head and reach for the sky. After several breaths bring the right foot back to the floor. Repeat on the left side.

Sanskrit Yoga Name:
VRKSASANA

Snow Cat

Start on your hands and knees, with your shoulders directly above your hands. Keep your arms straight. Exhale and arch your back to the sky, drop your head down and pull in your tummy. Inhale, flatten your back, push out your tummy and lift your head back up.

Sanskrit Yoga Name:
BIDALASANA

Lion

Kneel on the floor, lean forward and place both hands on the floor besides your knees. Keep your back straight. As you exhale stretch forward lifting your bottom of the floor. Stick out your tounge and give a huge roar!

Sanskrit Yoga Name:
SIMHASANA

Butterfly

Sit on your bottom with the soles of your feet together. Let your knees drop down towards the floor. Sit up straight and flap your legs like butterfly wings.

Sanskrit Yoga Name:
ARDHA-MATSYENDRASANA

Puppet

Stand with your feet hip width apart. Inhale and reach your arms up high Exhale and fold forwards at the hip, reaching towards the floor.

Sanskrit Yoga Name:
UTTANASANA

Bunny

Start on your hands and knees, with your hands directly below your shoulders. Tuck your toes under and push your bottom up to the sky. Gently soften your elbows and drop your head between your arms. Jump both feet off the floor with little bunny hops.

Bunny hops prepare
the body for handstands

Sanskrit Yoga Name:
ADHO MUKHA VRKSASANA

Down Dog

Start on your hands and knees, with your hands directly below your shoulders. Tuck your toes under and push your bottom up to the sky. until your arms and legs are straight. Relax your neck and try to push your heels into the ground.

Sanskrit Yoga Name:
ADHO MUKHA SAVNASANA

Owl

Sit on your bottom with your right leg crossed in front of your left leg. Inhale, sit up straight. Exhale, twist your body to the right and look down over your right shoulder.

Give a little hoot. Twist back to the front and repeat on the left side.

Sanskrit Yoga Name:
BADDHA KONASANA

Mouse

Kneel on the floor.
Sit your bottom onto your heels and fold forward putting your forehead onto the floor. Rest your arms beside your body on the floor, palms facing upwards.
Breathe deep and slow and let your sholders relax.

Sanskrit Yoga Name:
BALASANA

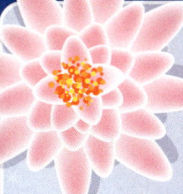
Sleeping Lotus

Lie on your back with your eyes closed, arms by your sides, palms facing upwards. Be completely relaxed and think about your happy thoughts. Feel your tummy rise as you inhale and fall as you exhale.

Sanskrit Yoga Name:
SAVASANA